What's a City Council?

First Guide to Government

Nancy Harris

Heinemann Library
Chicago, IL

©2008 Heinemann Library
a division of Reed Elsevier Inc.
Chicago, Illinois

Customer Service **888-454-2279**

Visit our website at **www.heinemannlibrary.com**

Photo research by Tracy Cummins and Tracey Engel
Designed by Kimberly R. Miracle and Betsy Wernert
Printed in China by South China Printing Company

11 10 09 08 07
10 9 8 7 6 5 4 3 2 1

ISBN-10: 1-4034-9509-2 (hc)   1-4034-9515-7 (pb)

Library of Congress Cataloging-in-Publication Data
Harris, Nancy, 1956-
  What's a city council? / Nancy Harris.
    p. cm. -- (First guide to government)
Includes bibliographical references and index.
ISBN-13: 978-1-4034-9509-9 (hc)
ISBN-13: 978-1-4034-9515-0 (pb)
1. City councils--United States--Juvenile literature. 2. Municipal government--United States--Juvenile literature. I. Title.
JS346.H36 2008
       320.8'54--dc22

Acknowledgments
The author and publishers are grateful to the following for permission to reproduce copyright material: ©Alamy **p. 17** (Glow Images); ©AP Photo **pp. 10** (Mary Godleski), **12** (M. Spencer Green), **13** (Wide World Photos), **15** (Paul Sakuma), **18** (Richard Drew), **21** (Steve Helber), **25** (Wide World Photos), **26** (Wide World Photos), **27** (Ozier Muhammad, Pool); ©Courtesy Atlanta City Council **pp. 11, 22, 29**; ©CORBIS **p. 7** (Owaki/Kulla); ©Getty Images **pp. 6** (Giulio Marcocchi), **24** (Panoramic Images); ©Image Works **pp. 4** (Bob Daemmrich), **14** (Bob Daemmrich), **23** (Amsterdam Recorder/Mitch Wojnarowicz); ©Redux **pp. 16** (The New York Times/Robert Spencer), **28** (The Boston Globe/John Tlumacki); ©Shutterstock **p. 9** (top image: Anne Kitzman; bottom image: Mario Savoia); ©ZUMA Press **p. 19** (Minneapolis Star Tribune/ Bruce Bisping).

Cover photography reproduced with permission of age fotostock/SuperStock.

Every effort has been made to contact copyright holders of any material reproduced in this book. Any omissions will be rectified in subsequent printings if notice is given to the publisher.

Contents

Some words are shown in bold, **like this**. You can find out what they mean by looking in the glossary.

Governments in the United States

The United States has different levels of governments. The United States **federal government** makes decisions for the whole country.

★ People vote to choose leaders in government.

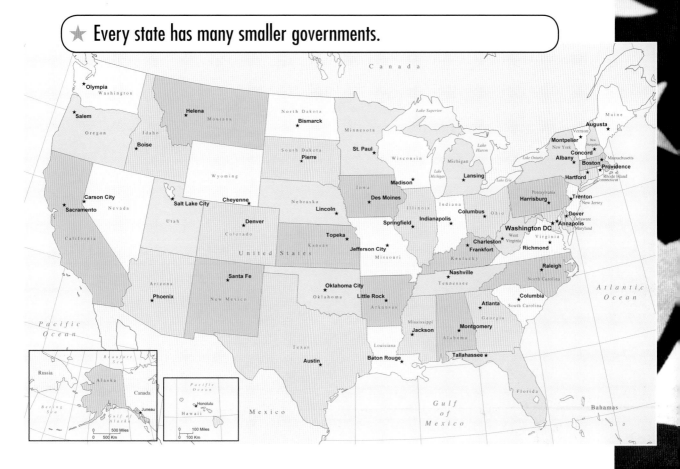

Each state has its own government. The state government makes decisions for the whole state.

There are also smaller governments in each state. These governments make decisions for their city or town. A city council is part of these governments.

What Is a City Council?

★ The city council meets often to discuss how to run the city.

A city council is a group of people **elected** (chosen) to represent the people in a city. **Citizens** in each city vote to decide who should serve on the council. City council members must live in the area where they serve.

★ The city council meets inside the City Hall.

City council members make decisions for people who live in their area of the state. They are in charge of important services. Some of these services help keep people in the city safe.

What Is a Municipal Government?

A city council is part of a **municipal government** in a state. A municipal government makes decisions for a small area within a state.

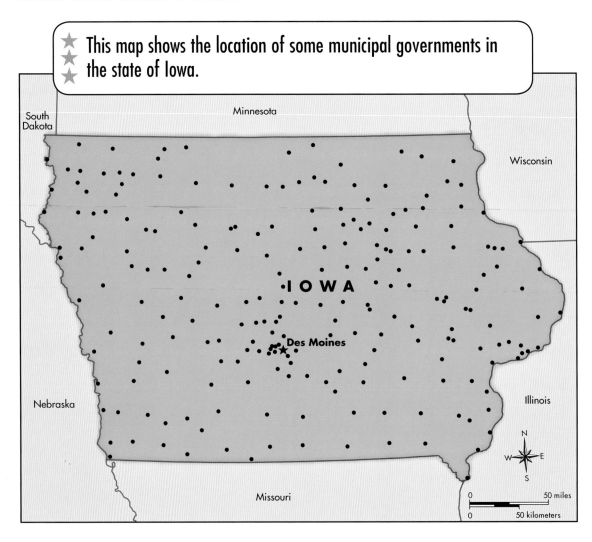

This map shows the location of some municipal governments in the state of Iowa.

Small river town in Kentucky

New York City

⭐ Municipal areas are many different sizes.

A **municipal area** could be a city, town, or village. Some municipal areas are very large, such as New York City. Others can be very small.

What Is the Role of the City Council?

The city council is the **legislative** part of a city government. It makes the **laws** for the city. Laws are rules people must follow.

★★★ This is council member Eugene Robinson of Atlanta, Georgia. He is discussing a new law.

★ Council members vote to make decisions.

City council members have other jobs. They include:

- **committee** (group) decisions
- **budget** (money) decisions.

Making Laws

It takes many steps to make a city **law**. First someone thinks of an idea for a law. Then a city council member must write a report about the idea. The report is called a **bill**.

★ Council members present bills in meetings.

City council members look at the bill and discuss it. People in **committees** or groups that are **affected** by the bill also review it. For example, a bill on education would be discussed by the education committee members.

★ Council members discuss bills together.

Citizens in the city can also discuss the **bill**. This happens in meetings set up at certain times. During these meetings, people can share their ideas on a bill with city council members.

★★★ Citizens can attend meetings to discuss matters of the city council.

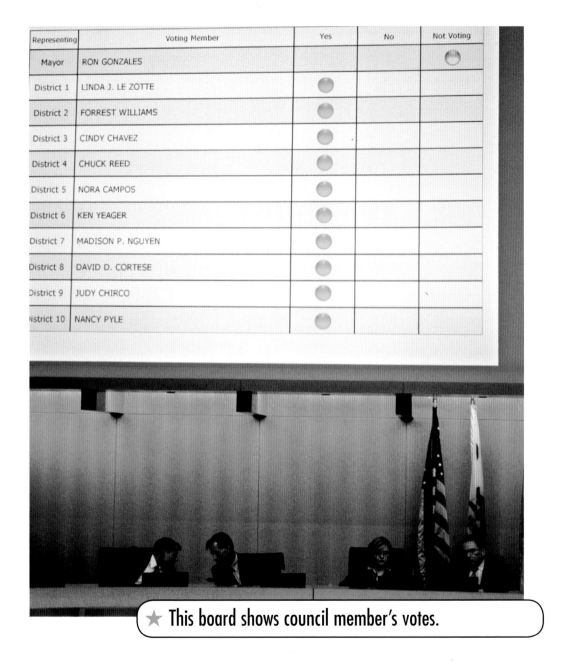

Representing	Voting Member	Yes	No	Not Voting
Mayor	RON GONZALES			○
District 1	LINDA J. LE ZOTTE	○		
District 2	FORREST WILLIAMS	○		
District 3	CINDY CHAVEZ	○		
District 4	CHUCK REED	○		
District 5	NORA CAMPOS	○		
District 6	KEN YEAGER	○		
District 7	MADISON P. NGUYEN	○		
District 8	DAVID D. CORTESE	○		
District 9	JUDY CHIRCO	○		
District 10	NANCY PYLE	○		

★ This board shows council member's votes.

City council members then vote on the bill. In many cities, the bill is sent to the **mayor** after the city council **approves** it.

★
★
★
People who are **affected** by the bill are invited
to watch the mayor sign it.

The **mayor** is the leader of a city or town. If the mayor
signs the **bill**, it becomes a **law**.

Washington, D.C.

★ The federal government is in Washington, D.C.

People in the city must follow these laws. They must also follow laws made by their state government and the United States **federal government**.

City Council Committees

JETS		CABLEVISION	
+ $280 million	Jets	$400 million	Cablevi
- $751 million	Taxpayers	+$0 million	T
-$471million		+$400 million	
	$871 million	Taxpayer	
+	$300 million	Lost Valu	
TOTAL	$1.175 billion	Taxpayers	

★ Committees help make decisions for the city.

City councils have many **committees**. These are small groups of people with similar knowledge or interests. Each committee has a specific job. For example, one committee makes decisions about health care.

Some of the committees include:

- education
- safety
- streets and services (roads)
- zoning (what can be built and where).

⭐ One committee decides when roads need to be fixed.

City councils in large cities have many **committees**. All city councils have committees that meet regularly. Some cities have additional committees that only meet for a short time when a special issue needs to be discussed.

★ This is a list of some of the committees that a city may have.

COMMITTEE NAME	JOB
Aviation	In charge of airports
Budget	In charge of the city's money and how it is spent
Public Utilities	In charge of waste removal and recycling programs
Transportation	In charge of maintaining buses, subways, and streets
Special Events	In charge of parades, festivals, and neighborhood parties
Police and Fire	In charge of the police and fire departments

Committee members must work together to make decisions.

The city council members work with each committee. Sometimes they make decisions for the committees. Sometimes they choose committee leaders.

★
★
★ Council members review information given to them by committees.

Sometimes city council members are on **committees**. They go to committee meetings and share decisions made by other city council members.

Budget Decisions

★★★ City council members meet together to make plans for the city budget.

One job of the city council is to make decisions about the city's **budget**. They decide how much money is needed to run the city.

The money is used to run all the parts of the **municipal government**. For example, the money is used to run the **committees**. It may also be used to repair city roads or put up traffic signals.

Some budget money may go to building new public places in the city.

This is Mayor Bloomberg of New York City. He is discussing how much money will go to toward the city's schools.

In some cities, the city council plans the **budget**. In other cities, the **mayor** of the city creates the budget.

Citizens can meet and share their ideas with city leaders.

The **budget** is discussed by the city council members and **committees**. It can also be discussed by the **citizens** of the city. Citizens can discuss the budget with city council members at meetings.

The budget can be changed during these meetings. After the meetings, the city council looks over the budget and **approves** it.

★ These council members are talking about their city's budget.

Running for City Council

There are **laws** that tell who can run for city council. There are also laws that tell how long a person can serve on a city council. These rules are different in each state.

★ People running for city council meet with
★ **citizens** to discuss their needs.

City councils are very important. They make the laws for the city. They make decisions on how the city should be run.

★ Council members work together to lead our cities.

Glossary

affected changed by

approve agree to

bill written proposal or idea for a new law

budget list of money needed to run each part of the city's government

citizen person who is born in the United States. People who have moved to the United States from another country can become citizens by taking a test.

committee group of people who work together to do a specific job

elect choose a leader by voting

federal government group of leaders who run the entire country. In a federal government, the country is made up of many states.

law rule people must obey in a state or country

legislative branch part of the city government that makes laws

mayor leader in a municipal government

municipal area small area within a state, such as a city, town, or village

municipal government group of leaders who run a small area in a state

More Books to Read

De Capua, Sarah. *Making a Law*. New York: Children's Press, 2004.

DeGezelle, Terri. *The City Council*. Mankato, MN: Capstone Press. 2005.

Web Sites

Great Government for Kids has information about local government, state governments, and the federal government.
http://www.cccoe.net/govern/index.html

Visit PBS Kids' the Democracy Project to play fun games and learn all about how local, state, and federal governments run your city or town.
http://pbskids.org/democracy/mygovt/police.html

Index